CONTENTS

MILL

FROM COTTAGE TO MILL

Take a look at a Victorian mill town. It is almost six o'clock on a dark and chilly October morning. A young girl, no more than ten years old, is hurrying to the cotton mill. Her clogs clatter on the cobbled street. She looks up at the tall building that will imprison her until the evening. There are long rows of grimy windows that let light into the mill, but they have frosted glass to stop the workers looking out.

▲ Swainson Birley Mill, painted in 1834.

'Sixty years ago there was not a cotton mill in these parts; at present there are no fewer than sixty-five.'[1]

At the start of the nineteenth century, the cotton industry was booming. Rich bankers and merchants were eager to build cotton mills and fill them with spindles and looms. The many new mills were given nicknames by local people. Swainson Birley Mill in Preston became known as 'The big 'un'. Other mills, such as the 'Puff-n-dart' and 'Bang-the-nation', were named after the steam engines that powered them.

In 1804, William Blake wrote a poem which spoke of the 'dark Satanic mills' spreading across the English landscape.[2]

▲ Armley Mill at Leeds, in Yorkshire, as it looks today. Look at the many windows.

For centuries, British cloth had been made not from cotton but from sheep's wool. Merchants delivered wool from local farms to the cottages of the workers. They cleaned the wool in urine, spun it into yarn on a spinning wheel, then used a hand loom to weave the yarn into cloth.

◀ A nineteenth-century spinster.

Families shared this work. The women who did the spinning were known as 'spinsters'. Their husbands and sons wove the spun thread. The finished cloth was collected by the merchants and carried away on their pack horses. Children were expected to help with this family industry, which was known as the Domestic System.

◀ A spinning wheel made in 1770.

The growing population needed more and more clothes. Machines were invented to produce cloth more quickly, but they were too large to be used in workers' homes. The next step was to collect workers and machinery together under one roof. In 1771, Richard Arkwright set up the first modern mill, at Cromford, in Derbyshire.

▶ This machine was used in Arkwright's mill.

COTTON

A NEW MATERIAL

In a cloud of dust, two men struggle to wheel a huge bale of raw cotton through the mill gates. Children push past them, as the clang of the mill bell signals the start of the working day. Breakfast will not be served until the workers have been at their machines for three hours.

'The yarn spun in this country would, in a single thread, pass round the globe's circumference 203,775 times; it would reach 51 times from the earth to the sun, and it would encircle the earth's orbit eight and a half times.'[3]

▲ Taking a cotton bale to the mill.

▲ An American steamboat loaded with bales of raw cotton.

At the end of the eighteenth century, there was a growing fashion for a light, exotic cloth made in India. It was made from the seed-heads of cotton plants, which have thin hairs or fibres that can be spun into a thread.

An enormous amount of cotton was picked by slaves working on plantations in America. The raw cotton was cleaned, then pressed into square bags called bales. Thousands of these bales were sent to Liverpool by ship, and taken to the new mills by road or canal.

At the mill, raw cotton had to be prepared before it could be spun. First, it was cleaned by beating or 'scutching' to remove dust. A process called 'willowing' then separated the cotton fibres. Next, these tangled fibres were combed or 'carded' to make them lie straight. This was originally done by hand, using wire-toothed brushes or 'cards'.

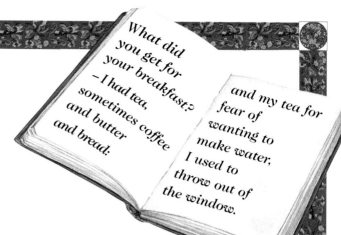

What did you get for your breakfast? – I had tea, sometimes coffee and butter and bread; and my tea for fear of wanting to make water, I used to throw out of the window.

▲ Women carding at Swainson Birley Mill in 1834.

In the first mills there were water-powered carding engines which both carded and twisted the cotton. It could then be spun into thread on machines called 'water frames'.

'It is by iron fingers, teeth and wheels, moving with exhaustless energy and devouring speed, that the cotton is opened, cleaned, spread, carded, drawn, roved, spun, wound, warped, dressed and woven.'[4]

▲ A carding engine from 1830.

WATERWHEELS AND ENGINES

The deafening noise of machinery suddenly goes quiet. The giant waterwheel that powers the mill has stopped turning. Millwrights hurry outside to make repairs. They are perhaps the most important workers in the mill. This does not stop the owner shouting after them: 'I'll have that steam engine soon, then you'll all be out of a job!'

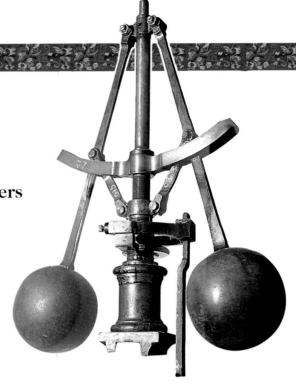

▲ This machine controlled the flow of water to the wheel.

▲ A waterwheel providing the mill's power.

The first mills were built on the banks of fast-flowing rivers. They had waterwheels, which were turned by the river rushing into their buckets or paddles. This generated power, which was transmitted to each floor of the mill by iron shafts and gears.

Waterwheels relied on the steady flow of the river. At Quarry Bank Mill, in Cheshire, the River Bollin was dammed each night to increase power for the following day. Eleven waterwheels on the River Clyde drove the looms at Scotland's New Lanark Mills. Droughts and floods could be disastrous. Up to twenty working days were lost each year at Dewsbury Mills, Yorkshire, when the River Calder flooded its banks.

▶ A pressure gauge from Armley Mill.

'The water ... depends much on the dams of the mills on the stream above ... we use the water when it comes down to us. We cannot work frequently in summer before ten or eleven o'clock a.m. and must work in the evening as long as the supply of water lasts.'[5]

Steam engines, developed by James Watt in the 1780s, gradually replaced the waterwheel. By 1830, eighty per cent of cotton spinning was powered by steam. Mills could now be built far from rivers, in towns where there were plenty of available workers.

Is not the place full of steam? – Yes; and the machinery throws off water perpetually; so that we are wet to the skin by the hot water.

'There was a rattling and a trembling all day long where the piston of the steam engine worked ... up and down like the head of an elephant in a state of melancholy madness.'[6]

▲ These mechanics looked after the steam engine at Quarry Bank Mill, in 1890.

Cotton towns like Preston, Glasgow and Blackburn grew up around the mills. The biggest was Manchester, which became known as 'Cottonopolis'. Its population increased at an alarming rate, from 25,000 in 1772 to 455,000 in 1851. Workers were housed in overcrowded slums, stained with soot from the mills' smoking chimneys.

▲ A mill engineer's oil can.

BRUSH

DUST FROM THE MULES

Inside the spinning room, the air is stale. One woman brushes the machinery, stirring up a choking cloud of cotton fibres from the whirring cogs. Fluff clings to her hair and clothes, and makes her eyes sting. The woman coughs and wheezes as she tries to catch her breath. She spits into the handkerchief clutched to her nose, and her spit is full of blood.

▶ A woman brushes cotton dust from the moving machinery.

▼ The cogs and chains of machines were very dangerous.

Many cotton workers suffered breathing problems. In the winter, they left the intense heat of the mills and walked home in the icy cold. Such changes in temperature, and the constant breathing of cotton dust and steam in the air, ruined their lungs. Diseases such as pneumonia were common.

▲ A brush used to clean machinery.

'The air is filled with fibrous dust, which produces chest infection especially among workers in the carding and combing rooms. The most common effects of this breathing of dust are blood-spitting, hard noisy breath, pains in the chest, coughs, sleeplessness ... ending in the worst cases of consumption.'[7]

Look inside a Victorian mill and you will see rows of machines called 'spinning mules'. The mule had been invented in 1779, by Samuel Crompton. It combined the ideas of two older machines, the spinning jenny and the water frame. Crompton's mule could operate large numbers of bobbins at once, producing strong, fine thread very quickly.

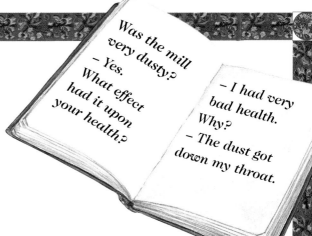

Was the mill very dusty?
– Yes.
What effect had it upon your health?

– I had very bad health.
Why?
– The dust got down my throat.

Workers brushed dust from the mules while they were in motion. There were no safety guards, and they had to crawl under and reach into sharp, fast-moving gears and cogs. There were many accidents. Workers became careless at the end of the day, exhausted by hunger, heat and long hours watching the hypnotic movements of the machines.

◀ A boy cleans under the mules.

Workers maimed by mill machinery were a common sight in Manchester. In 1842, a woman caught her skirt in a cogwheel, and was dragged into the machinery and killed.

◀ Machinery at Armley Mill.

▼ Bobbins from a spinning mule.

'A great number of maimed ones may be seen going about in Manchester; this one has lost an arm or part of one, that one a foot ... it is like living in the midst of an army just returned from campaign.'[8]

WORKERS

LONG, HOT DAYS

The mill manager gathers all his female workers together. They wear long skirts, thick sacking pinafores and grey shawls. He tells them that there was an accident yesterday, when a woman's hair became caught in a mule's cogs. He says that any worker who fails to tie up her hair in future will be fined.

▲ A machine cog.

Two-thirds of the mill workers were women and children. The mill owner found them cheaper, and easier to control. Under the Domestic System, they had worked in their own homes, at their own pace. In the mills, they had to work at the constant rate of the power-driven machines.

◀ Mill workers in 1900.

Entire families worked in the mill. They laboured from six in the morning until eight at night, with a ten-minute break for breakfast, one hour for lunch, and twenty minutes for tea. Returning home at night, they were too exhausted to bother much with cooking or washing.

'Mr. T. Ashton employs 1,500 workpeople of both sexes. One immense room, filled with looms, contains 400 of them. The young women are well and decently clothed. A sort of large apron, extending from the shoulders to the feet, protects their outer garments from dirt.'[9]

▲ Spinning at Dean Mills in 1851.

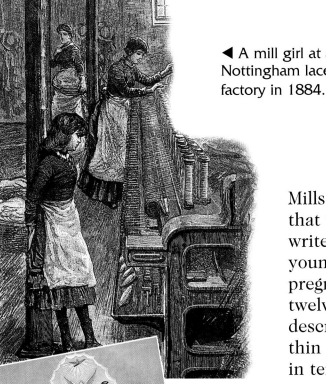

*Did that labour fatigue you very much?
– Yes: You found yourself very much tired?*

– Yes, as soon as I went home and sat down by the fire I fell asleep.

◄ A mill girl at a Nottingham lace factory in 1884.

Mills needed to be kept hot and damp so that the cotton threads did not snap. One writer visited a Glasgow cotton mill where young women workers, some of them pregnant, had to stand for twelve hours a day. He described them as pale, thin and barefoot, working in terrible heat and stink.

'So men and women all of you,
Come and buy a song or two,
And assist us to subdue,
    The Cotton Lords of Preston ...
    Oh then we'll dance and sing with glee,
    And thank you all right heartily,
    When we gain the victory,
        And beat the Lords of Preston.'[10]

▲ Trade union members were given certificates like this one.

► A mill girl in 1887.

Workers formed trade unions to demand better wages and conditions. In 1853, mill workers in Preston went on strike for thirty-six weeks, seeking a ten per cent pay rise. They sold copies of songs like the one above to raise funds.

WARNING SIGN

ACCIDENTS AND LOOMS

In the weaving shed, there are row upon row of massive power looms. An engineer examines one machine that has broken down. Behind him, two weavers try to talk to each other. The rattle of the shuttles and groan of the drive-belts make such a deafening racket that they have to lip-read to be able to understand each other.

▲ Power loom workers at Swainson Birley.

Warning signs nailed to the walls told workers that they would receive no compensation for injuries. Mill owners blamed terrible accidents on workers' carelessness, and refused to fence off the sharp, moving parts of machines. Workers severed fingers, or were 'scalped' when their hair became entangled. The moving parts of machines glowed red-hot. Many workers suffered burns, and a number of mills were burnt to the ground by sparks.

WARNING
CLIMBING OVER MULE HEADSTOCKS IS STRICTLY PROHIBITED.
THE MANAGEMENT WILL TAKE EXCEPTION TO ANY CLAIM FOR COMPENSATION FOR ACCIDENTS ARISING FROM THIS IRREGULARITY
BY ORDER.

▲ A warning sign from Armley Mill.

'I was working and there was a great deal of cotton in the machine; one of the wheels caught my finger and tore it off ... I was attended by the Surgeon of the factory Mr Holland and in about six weeks I recovered.'[11]

▲ A shuttle from a loom.

Once it had been spun, the cotton was ready to be woven into cloth. With mules spinning more and more thread, weavers using the old hand looms could not keep up. A solution lay in the power loom, invented in 1786 by a vicar named Dr Edmund Cartwright. By 1829, there were 49,000 power looms in the mills.

Had any of them any accident? – Yes, my eldest daughter ... the cog caught her forefinger nail, and screwed it off below the knuckle, and she was five weeks in Leeds Infirmary.

'Should any dire calamity befall the land of cotton [America], a thousand of our merchant ships would rot idly in dock; ten thousand mills must stop their busy looms; two thousand mouths would starve.'[12]

Weavers supervised two to four looms at a time. The noise was deafening and they had nothing to protect their hearing. One woman claimed she could not sleep at night because the roar of the machines stayed in her head.

▲ Yorkshire weavers at their looms.

A writer observed that the working life of a power loom weaver was passed amid a noise like an express train passing through a tunnel. At Quarry Bank Mill, the vibrations of the machines caused damage to the building itself.

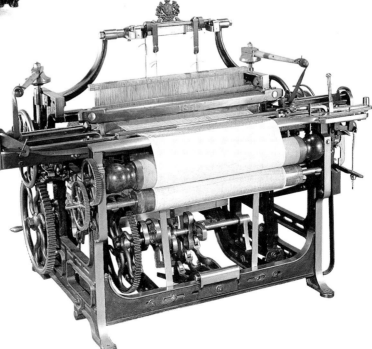

▶ This power loom was made in 1851.

SCAVENGERS

THE MILL CHILDREN

Amid the cotton dust and whirring bobbins of the spinning mules, tiny children go about their different tasks. A filthy, ragged boy known as a 'scavenger' crawls beneath the mules, picking up fluff. A 'doffer' lifts out bobbins full of cotton and replaces them with empty ones. A girl known as a 'piecer' sleepily knots together a broken thread in the heart of the flying reels.

▶ A piecer mending threads.

'I was first employed to doff bobbins ... I used to oil the machinery every morning ... I was obliged to make overtime every night but I did not like this as I wanted to learn my book. We had school every night but we used to attend about once a week.'[13]

▶ Few mills had children's chairs, like this one from Armley.

▲ A bobbin made into a simple toy.

Thousands of children, some as young as four, worked in the mills. Many were paupers and orphans, sent to the mills of Lancashire and Yorkshire to be taken on as apprentices. Others worked in the mill with their parents. Some mill children received only eighteen pence a week in 1831, but the mill provided food which their parents could not otherwise afford.

One mill owner noted how his doffers spent the whole day bent double over their machines, and never quite straightened up again. Another said of the mill children: 'Many of them became dwarfs in body and mind, and some of them were deformed.'

Children's work was exhausting. A piecer could walk twenty miles in a twelve hour shift. Some fell asleep on the mill floor. Conditions improved slowly. After the Factory Act of 1833, it became illegal for a child under the age of nine to work in the mill.

▼ A twelve-hour day was too long for many children to stay awake.

▲ Lancashire mill girls, around 1900.

After 1847, no-one under the age of eighteen was allowed to work more than a ten-hour day. How would you feel about working from 8 am until 6 pm?

'I have seen them fall asleep, and they have been performing their work with their hands while they were asleep ... going through the motion of piecing fast asleep, when there was really no work to do.'[14]

INDENTURE

THE APPRENTICE HOUSE

One of the older boys is called into the manager's office, and told that he is to be made an apprentice tailor. He will receive training and three shillings a week, but will have to work at the mill for the next six years. The manager tells him to sign a contract called an 'indenture'. The boy peers at it, but he has never learned to read or write.

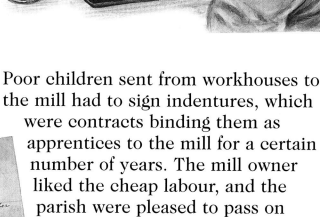

▶ The manager presents an apprentice with his indenture.

'This indenture witnesses that John Metcalfe does put himself Apprentice unto the full end and term of six years ... his Master faithfully shall serve, his secrets keep, his lawful commands everywhere gladly do ... He shall not haunt taverns or playhouses nor absent himself from his said Master's service day or night.'[15]

Poor children sent from workhouses to the mill had to sign indentures, which were contracts binding them as apprentices to the mill for a certain number of years. The mill owner liked the cheap labour, and the parish were pleased to pass on the cost of feeding the children.

At the end of the day, up to one hundred exhausted children slept in the mill's apprentice house. At Litton Mill, Derbyshire, boys and girls slept in one room, six to each bunk.

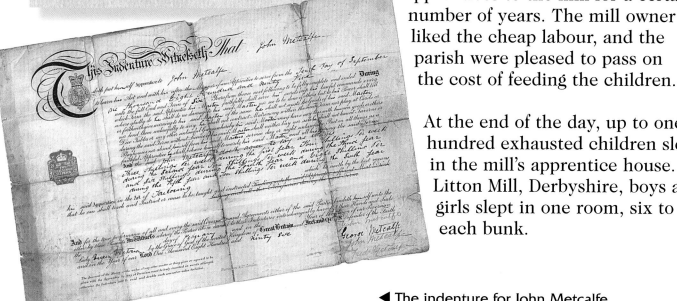

◀ The indenture for John Metcalfe, an apprentice tailor in 1895.

▲ Inkwells from the school at Armley Mill.

Had you sometimes to clean the machinery at your dinner hour? – Yes, and to wipe all the machines.

How long did that take you generally? – About a quarter of an hour, and sometimes twenty minutes.

Mill owners were supposed to provide schools, but many apprentices found themselves cleaning toilets and tending the mill garden instead of studying. Those that ran away were pursued and caught. They had their hair cut off as punishment, and were returned to the apprentice house.

▶ This man supervised apprentices working in the garden at Quarry Bank.

▲ A dancing display at Robert Owen's New Institution in 1825.

Some apprentices were luckier. At New Lanark Mills, near Glasgow, Robert Owen abolished corporal punishment. He set up the first infants' classes and built a school called the New Institution. Children under ten did not work, and older children worked short hours, so that they were not too tired to study.

A teacher at Robert Owen's New Institution said that there were 'dancing masters, a fiddler, a band of music, that there were drills and exercises and that [the children] were dancing together till they were more fatigued than if they were working.'[16]

TOP HAT

OVERSEERS AND INSPECTORS

When two men in top hats enter the mill, the apprentices go about their work with greater speed. One of the men is a factory inspector. The other, who carries a stick with knotted thongs, is the overseer responsible for watching over the workers. He is careful not to strike or speak harshly to the apprentices. That will change once the inspector has left.

▶ The overseer, ready to punish any lazy workers.

▲ An overseer at work in a mill in 1853.

In many mills, any children who were lazy, misbehaved or made mistakes were severely beaten with a strap. Parents often had to witness their own children being treated cruelly. They were in desperate need of the family wage and did not dare complain, in case they were sacked.

▲ The mill overseer's top hat.

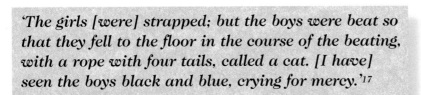

'The girls [were] strapped; but the boys were beat so that they fell to the floor in the course of the beating, with a rope with four tails, called a cat. [I have] seen the boys black and blue, crying for mercy.'[17]

Overseers carried leather thongs or heavy iron sticks called 'billy-rollers'. They beat children to keep them awake and alert towards the end of a long day. Some overseers threw water in the children's faces. Others gave them a pinch of snuff, to make them sneeze.

Is it a common thing for you children to be beaten? – Yes, there used to be screaming among the boys and girls every time of the day, and they made black and blue marks on their shoulders.

Commissioners were sent by Parliament to investigate the terrible conditions in the mills. They interviewed workers, and published their reports in Blue Books like the one above. This led to Acts of Parliament being passed that reduced working hours. Factory inspectors visited mills to make sure that the new laws were obeyed.

▲ An inspector interviews Leeds mill girls in 1860.

One overseer told an inspector: 'I was sometimes obliged to chastise [children] when they were almost fainting, and it hurt my feelings; then they would spring up and work pretty well for another hour; but the last two or three hours were my hardest work, for they then got so exhausted.'[18]

JAMES TATE. MAKER
TATE'S
PATENT.
BRADFORD

◀ A machine panel from Armley Mill.

Many of the conditions described in this book were common at the beginning of Queen Victoria's reign in 1837. Acts of Parliament gradually improved conditions, but there were never enough factory inspectors to enforce the laws everywhere. By 1900, though, harsh punishments, long hours and child labour had disappeared from most mills.

▲ An overseer watching his women workers.

WAGE TOKEN

THE COUNTING HOUSE

There is a buzz of excitement, as a clerk from the counting house pushes his rattling trolley in through the door of the weaving shed. It is loaded with cups full of money, each with a number stamped on it. A weaver gives a numbered token to the clerk, and is handed the cup containing his wages. He tips a few coins into his hand then continues shaking the empty cup, to the amusement of the other weavers.

▲ A wage token.

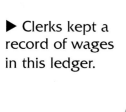

► Clerks kept a record of wages in this ledger.

▲ The wages clerk and his trolley were a welcome sight for the workers.

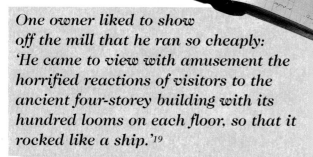

One owner liked to show off the mill that he ran so cheaply: 'He came to view with amusement the horrified reactions of visitors to the ancient four-storey building with its hundred looms on each floor, so that it rocked like a ship.'[19]

On a Wednesday, in the mill's counting house, a bookkeeper and two clerks calculated the workers' wages. Money was taken off for the rent of the workers' cottages, purchases from the mill store, loan repayments and fines for being late.

In one cotton mill, the clerks worked in silence from 7 am until 6 pm. They wrote their calculations in the accounts book, and the wages trolley made its rounds on Fridays.

Many mills had their own stores. Some, known as 'tommy-shops', sold poor quality goods at high prices. Workers were sacked if they did not spend their wages there. This practice, known as the 'truck system', was stopped by mill owners such as Robert Owen.

'The door of Mr Diggs' tommy-shop opened ... Guarded by rails from all contact, sat Mr Diggs senior ... recommending his ... customers to be patient.'[20]

▲ Factory girls in Wigan enjoying their lunch.

▲ The stores at Owen's New Lanark Mills.

At lunchtime, workers were given porridge, potatoes, and sometimes bacon. At one Derbyshire mill, the provisions were guarded by an old man armed with a stick! Some workers went to the store for lunch. At New Lanark, Robert Owen opened a store where his workers could swap tokens for cheap, high quality goods.

MILL OWNER

IMPROVING CONDITIONS

In his comfortable office, the mill owner reads over a letter that he has received from a fellow cotton manufacturer. The letter says that some owners are reducing the hours worked by the people in their mills. They believe that this stops the workers becoming tired, and they produce more cloth. Profits then increase. The mill owner begins to chuckle. He screws up the paper and hurls it into the bin.

▲ Robert Owen, painted in 1834.

▲ Villagers at New Lanark in 1890.

Robert Owen said of the people working at New Lanark when he took over the mill: 'Theft and the receipt of stolen goods was their trade, idleness and drunkenness their habit.'[21]

At New Lanark, Robert Owen gave his workers 'silent monitors'. These coloured pieces of wood showed how workers were performing: black (bad), blue (average), yellow (good) and white (excellent). Owen improved conditions and reduced hours. His happier workers worked harder, and increased his profits. Many mill owners refused to follow Owen's example until forced to by the Factory Acts.

▲ We still have many mill owners' papers, like these from Quarry Bank.

Owners made steady improvements
throughout the country. At Quarry Bank
Mill, in 1823, Samuel Greg opened a
school and village store. Greg's wife
Hannah helped to teach the apprentices,
and a doctor was appointed to check on
their health.

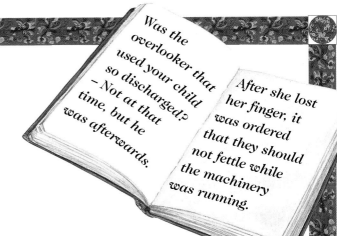

Was the overlooker that used your child so discharged? – Not at that time, but he was afterwards.

After she lost her finger, it was ordered that they should not fettle while the machinery was running.

◄ Samuel Greg, the owner of Quarry Bank Mill.

One mill owner, Sir Titus Salt,
was disgusted by the filth of
mill towns. In 1853, he built a
village around his mill at
Saltaire, in Yorkshire. Most
workers lived in cramped,
back-to-back terraces, but Salt
built large, comfortable houses
on wide streets. Salt also created
a church, school and riverside
park for the workers at his mill.

Workers sang a song in praise of Titus Salt:
'He hath built up a palace to Labour,
Will equal the Caesars of old,
The Church and the School and the Cottage,
And lavished his thousands of gold;
Where the workmen may live and be happy,
Enjoying the fruits of his hand,
Surrounded with comfort and plenty,
Secure as a peer of the land.'[22]

► The owner kept records written with quill and ink.

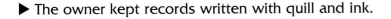

25

CLOCK

TIMEKEEPING AND FINES

Two spinners keep glancing up past the overseer to the clock on the wall. Its hands seem to move so slowly. When it shows eight o'clock, the mill bell will chime and they will hurry away from the heat, dust and noise. But that time never seems to come.

▶ Quarry Bank workers used this clocking-in clock.

▲ Workers winding bobbins in 1900.

The clock controlled the workers' lives. They had to clock-on in the morning and clock-off at night, by inserting a card into a special clock. Anyone who arrived late or left early, for whatever reason, was fined. The notice on the clock shown above promised workers the chance of 'inspecting the time booked at each operation, thus avoiding disputes at the weekend'.

Some employees were cheated by the mill owners. One worker, James Leach, wrote a book which revealed how owners deliberately altered the factory clock, by winding it forward when his workers left at night. When the workers arrived the following morning, the owner claimed that a large group of them were late. They were locked out of the mill, and fines were taken from their wages.

▲ A list of fines from the counting house at Quarry Bank Mill.

In the days of the Domestic System, families had made their own rules. Work was less hurried at the start of the week, but it became frantic as the merchant's visit on a Saturday drew closer. In the mills, though, employers were unsure how to control large groups of workers. So, they made strict rules and punished those that broke them with fines.

► An oil can.

Fines For Water-Foot Mill, 1851

– For any oil wasted or spilled on the floor, 2 pence each offence, besides paying for the value of the oil.
– Any person neglecting to oil at the proper times shall be fined 2 pence.

▼ Cotton bobbins.

– For any bobbins found on the floor, 1 pence for each bobbin.
– Any person bringing dirty bobbins will be fined 1 pence for each bobbin.

◄ Mill machinery.

'The Machinery shall be swept down every meal time. Workpeople shall wash themselves at least twice every week. Any found not washed will be fined 3 pence for each offence.'[23]

The clerks in the counting house kept a list of the fines. You might realise how young some workers were when you read that one girl was fined for 'terrifying S. Pearse with her ugly face.'

DYE BOTTLE

THE FINISHED CLOTH

The cloth from the weavers' looms is carried up to the printers. They load it on to giant rollers which lift it high into the rafters. The printers pour purple dye into their machines, and brush it evenly over the material. As the mill bell signals the end of the day, the cotton cloth emerges printed with flowered patterns.

◀ William Perkin's first bottle of mauve dye.

▼ Workers printing cotton cloth in Swainson Birley in 1834.

A mechanical printer was invented in 1783. It could print up to five different dyes in patterns that were etched on to copper cylinders. In 1856, William Perkin, an eighteen-year-old chemistry student, discovered by accident the first artificial dye. Before this, dyeing had been a long process which involved dipping the cloth in cow dung and water!

◀ The finished cloth was wrapped in bales with labels like this one.

Cotton cloth lasted well and was comfortable to wear. It could be washed, ironed and dyed. By the early 1800s, it had almost replaced wool and linen in shirts, underwear and dresses. Power looms also led to the introduction of mechanized carpet weaving.

'It was a town of machinery and tall chimneys, out of which ... serpents of smoke trailed themselves for ever and ever, and never got uncoiled. It had a black canal in it, and a river that ran purple with evil-smelling dye.'[24]

– When the mill stopped for good, we went to the house to our supper, which was the same as breakfast – onion porridge and dry oat-cake.

By the end of the nineteenth century, working conditions were much improved in the mills. Cotton products now made up half of all British exports.

▲ A carpet-shearing machine from 1832.

Victorian etiquette required different clothes for different times of the day. Rich women wore morning clothes, afternoon tea dresses and evening gowns. By 1900, middle class women had jobs and could also afford new fashions. The mules and looms of the cotton mills kept pace with demand.

'The luxury of some of the ladies' dresses is perfectly astounding.'[25]

◀ Fashions from October 1850.

GLOSSARY

Apprentices Young workers under the care of a master who teaches them his trade.

Bobbins Small pins on which thread is wound.

Chastise Punish, especially by beating.

Compensation Payment to make up for an injury.

Consumption A lung disease now known as tuberculosis.

Etiquette Rules of polite behaviour.

Fettle Clean or trim.

Fibres Thin threads of material.

Fibrous Containing thin threads.

Looms Machines that weave threads into cloth.

Overseer A supervisor or foreman.

Maimed Mutilated or disabled by an accident.

Millwrights Workers who designed and looked after the mill and its machines.

Parish A district of local government.

Paupers Poor people who depend on charity from public funds.

Plantations Large estates on which rich owners used slaves to grow cotton.

Pneumonia A lung disease which makes breathing difficult.

Shilling A coin equal to twelve old pence.

Shuttles Bobbins with pointed ends, used in a loom.

Slums Overcrowded, filthy streets of houses.

Snuff Ground tobacco, often sniffed in the nineteenth century.

Spindles Pins used in spinning for twisting and winding thread.

Trade Union A group of workers organized to protect their rights.

Workhouses Shelters where the poor received food and lodging in return for doing jobs.

Yarn Thread that has been spun.

FURTHER READING

BOOKS TO READ

A Victorian Factory, Lyn Gash and Sheila Watson (Wayland, 1995)

I Was There, The Industrial Revolution, John D. Clare (Bodley Head, 1993)

Let's Discover a Victorian Mill, Brian Milton (Franklin Watts, 2002)

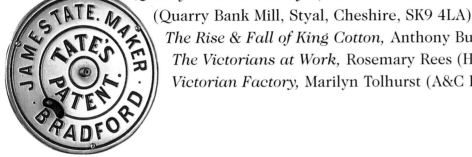

Quarry Bank Mill & Styal, Souvenir Guidebook (Quarry Bank Mill, Styal, Cheshire, SK9 4LA)

The Rise & Fall of King Cotton, Anthony Burton (BBC, 1997)

The Victorians at Work, Rosemary Rees (Heinemann, 1995)

Victorian Factory, Marilyn Tolhurst (A&C Black, 1996)

QUOTES

The Blue Book extracts in the book at the top of each spread come from interviews in the *Report of the Select Committee of Factory Children's Labour 1831-2.*

The other quotes from the mill can be found in the following sources:

1 Edward Baines, *History of the Cotton Manufacture in Great Britain,* 1835.
2 William Blake, *Jerusalem,* 1804.
3 Edward Baines.
4 Edward Baines.
5 Mill House Mill, in *Employment of Children in Factories,* 1834.
6 Charles Dickens, *Hard Times,* 1854.
7 Friedrich Engels, *Condition of the Working Classes in England in 1844.*
8 Friedrich Engels.
9 Leon Faucher, *Manchester in 1844.*
10 A popular ballad of 1853, in *The Rise and Fall of King Cotton,* Anthony Burton.
11 Thomas Priestley, age 13, in 1806.
12 E.N. Elliott, *Cotton is King and Pro-Slavery Arguments,* 1860.
13 Joseph Sefton, age 17, in 1806.
14 Commissioners, *Employment of Children in Factories,* 1833.
15 Indenture for an apprentice tailor, signed in 1895.
16 John Butt, *Industrial Archaeology of Scotland,* 1967.
17 Commissioners, *Employment of Children in Factories,* 1833.
18 Commissioners, *Employment of Children in Factories,* 1833.
19 A mill owner, quoted in *The Hungry Mills* by Norman Longmate, 1978.
20 Benjamin Disraeli, *Sybil,* 1846.
21 Robert Owen, quoted in *The Past All Around Us,* Reader's Digest 1979.
22 Traditional, 1870.
23 Rules in Water-Foot Mill, Haslingden, September 1851.
24 Charles Dickens, *Hard Times,* 1854.
25 *London Illustrated News,* 1864.

INDEX

Numbers in **bold** refer to pictures.